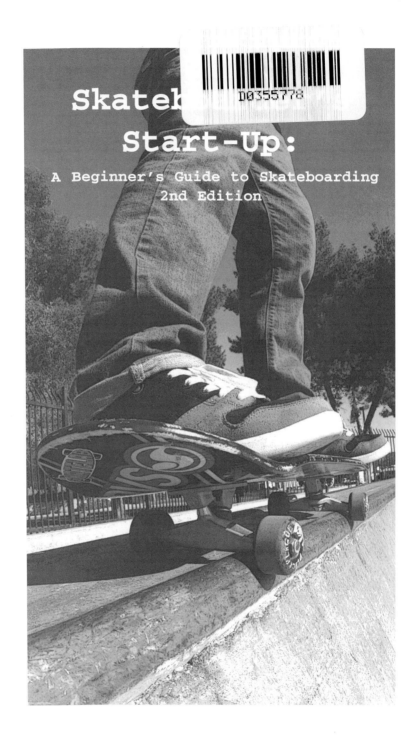

Skateb

Start-Up:

A Beginner's Guide to Skateboarding
2nd Edition

Steve Badillo

Skateboarder's Start-Up:

A Beginner's Guide to Skateboarding
2nd Edition

Doug Werner
Steve Badillo

Start-Up Sports®

Tracks Publishing
San Diego, California

Photography by Steve Badillo

Skateboarder's Start-Up:
A Beginner's Guide to Skateboarding
2nd Edition

Doug Werner
Steve Badillo

Start-Up Sports® / Tracks Publishing
140 Brightwood Avenue
Chula Vista, CA 91910
619-476-7125 Fax 619-476-8173
startupsports.com
trackspublishing.com

Copyright © 2009 by Doug Werner
1   2   3   4   5   6   7   8   9   10   11   12   13   14   15

Werner, Doug, 1950-
        Skateboarder's start-up : a beginner's guide to
    skateboarding / Doug Werner, Steve Badillo ; photography
    by Steve Badillo. – 2nd ed.
        p. cm. – (Start-up sports ; 11)
        Audience: Ages 12-25.
        ISBN-13: 9781884654343
        ISBN-10: 1884654347

        1. Skateboarding.   I. Badillo, Steve II. Title.
    III. Series: Start-up sports ; #11.

    GV859.8.W47 2009   796.22
                                  QBI09-1804

Dedicated
to SkateLab
— and to the spirit
of those who
built it

Acknowledgements

SkateLab
Camarillo Boys & Girls Skatepark
Oxnard Skatepark
The Cove Skatepark
Fillmore Skatepark
Santa Paula Skatepark
Becca Badillo
Gavin Badillo
Todd Huber
Alex Midler
Tom Schaar
Molly-Anne Dameron
Jack Ziehl
Riley Simone
Patrick Cannon
Gage Boyle
Devin Halliwell
Jackson Stern
Zach Lunchick
Michael Hanson
Noah Ruble
Scottie Radinski
Payson Gallager
Nick Oliver
Lilly Graves
Lexi Lunchick
Alek Richards
Leroy Grannis

Warning label

Beware, be safe and wear protective gear
When riders in this book are not wearing protective gear, it is only so that technique can be better captured in photographs. We do not condone skateboarding without protective equipment, and in fact, want to make it very clear that riders should wear helmet, elbow pads, knee pads and wrist guards to be as safe as possible.

It should be stated that skateboarding can be dangerous.
You will fall down as you learn. Riders should know and follow safe skateboarding procedure at all times.

Skateboarding means something different to everyone who comes to embrace it. It is a palette for your creativity, and diversity is its greatest attribute. For some it is a lifelong passion, lifestyle and struggle. For others it is an outlet to be enjoyed only once and awhile. Either way, skateboarding can progress with you as you progress with life. It provides a sense of accomplishment, and at the same time, leaves you wanting more. Skateboarding can be shared with others or be perfected alone, but its greatest meaning is in friendship. Those that continue to skate will continue to enjoy the special fellowship of skaters everywhere.

Steve Badillo

Our goal was to produce a guide that would introduce readers to skateboarding and impart fundamental technique. Apart from some videos, there isn't much that addresses basic skateboarding. In fact, there is a widespread belief that skating cannot be taught — the idea

being that young riders must suffer their lumps and simply learn by doing.

Although it's true there are lumps to suffer, it's ridiculous to think that skaters cannot enhance their learning through instructional material. Guides can generalize subject matter as well as break down and explain tricks. Sure, you need to learn by doing (it's called building muscle memory), but media (like this book) begins to tell you what and how to learn. The concept of instructional material is nothing new. What might be new is its place in the world of skating.

Doug Werner
Tracks

Contents

Gavin Badillo

intro

"People skate because of the rush, the traveling and the camaraderie.

Skateboarding is open and invites anyone to come into its culture and skate. There is no race or gender discrimination. The only thing that matters is your own ability and having fun."

—Steve Badillo

Skating = Personal expression

Why skate?

It's a bit difficult to explain the lure of skateboarding.

There are no rules. It's not a sport played between white lines. It's something different for everybody. It can be a simple or serious pursuit, a fun way to get around, or a dedicated lifestyle.

For most riders it provides moments of exhilaration and sweet freedom from the old day in, day out.

For many skaters it presents an ongoing *challenge* — a test of one's ability, mental toughness and fortitude.

Certainly it will alter your perception of the urban landscape. Everyday things and places on the street will have an exciting new meaning. And you will discover that skating is a global passion. You can travel almost anywhere and find skaters and places to ride.

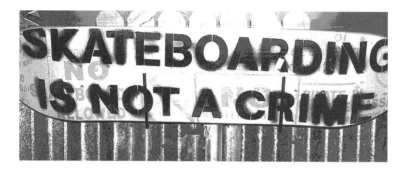

What's with the bad rap?

Skateboarding has never been embraced by the mainstream. At best, it has been tolerated, but for years it has reaped the scorn of a larger public that does not understand.

First and foremost, it is perceived to be a very dangerous activity. Dangerous to skaters and non-skaters alike. Second, skaters have been known to break laws associated with skateboarding and have at times shown a disrespect for public and private property. Add loud, aggressive music and (at times) outrageous fashions and you have a pill that few midlife citizens are willing to swallow — dangerous, law breaking, obnoxious young people on wheels.

Yet, it is also true that it's a New World.

Skateboarding is a hot commodity. Turn on your television and skateboarding is everywhere: Tony Hawk alongside Kobe Bryant and Michael Phelps in a commercial or Ryan Sheckler in his very own show. The bigger skateboarding events, such as ESPN X-Games, Van's Triple Crown of Skateboarding, Mountain Dew's Dew Tour and The Maloof Money Cup are now televised and viewed by millions all over the world.

More and more cities see skateboarding as a legitimate sport. They build and/or support the building of skate parks where skaters can skate away from pedestrians, traffic and unsafe riding surfaces. Laws are changing regarding the liability of park operators and the old excuse *We can't afford the insurance* is no longer valid.

Skateboarding's time has come. There are approximately 18.5 million skateboarders in the world presently, and they are supporting an estimated $5.7 billion business. Underneath the fears and misconceptions is an exciting sport and leisure activity that is as legit as Little League.

Ask any kid in the street.

Steve Badillo on skate culture

Steve Badillo is a sponsored professional skater and resident instructor at the world famous SkateLab Skatepark and Museum in Simi Valley, California. He's been a pro rider since 1993 and has taught thousands of people how to drop in. Steve was the technical adviser for this project. He and his students are the models for the photo sequences. He is a great coach and a true voice for skateboarding. His insights are placed throughout the text.

Why do skaters skate?

People skate because of the rush, the traveling and the camaraderie. Skateboarding is open and invites anyone to come into its culture and skate. There is no race or gender discrimination. The only thing that matters is your own ability and having fun.

What's the future of skateboarding?

The future of skateboarding is very positive. There are a lot of skate parks popping up all over the country and world. The level of professional skateboarding is so insane that it inspires everyone in and out of the skating universe. More and more skaters are getting better at a younger age. They are the future of this sport and embody the youthful spirit that makes skateboarding so appealing. Skateboarding can only grow.

Who are skateboarders?

Street skaters are urban guerrillas. And that's because we like to go out and skate everything in the street. But all that terrain is owned by someone. So when we skate the ledges of a bank, we get harassed by people that own the bank or by the police. Skating has been

illegal in a lot of cities. Even if you were to skate down the sidewalk, you can get a ticket or get your board confiscated. That has created an "us" versus "them" mentality.

In a way skateboarding is a sport for the everyday kid. It includes a very broad, diverse range of people —

Whites, Asians, Blacks, Mexicans — all kinds of people skateboarding. A lot of those people are not so well off — they're poor children who get skateboards and that's what they do. They don't get into football or anything else. They skateboard because it's free. They don't have to pay for it. They just go outside and start skating. It's not like that with other sports. There are certain obstacles that prohibit them from joining.

Society looks at these kids and makes judgements. They see them with their tattoos, they see that they are poor, they see them skating in front of banks or on downtown streets, and they think these kids are lowlifes.

Skateboarding has its own culture, dialect and fashion that is unique.

So the kids get labeled. We have been labeled since the beginning.

So we, in turn, have created our own skateboarding culture. We make it better for ourselves in spite of what other people think. We improve our place in the world in a variety of ways. We build skate parks. We do demos for the kids. We organize skate camps. There's actually a lot of positive things in skateboarding.

Why do you skate?

This is what gets me off:

When I go to a skate park, I look for the best skaters. Then I throw down my best moves and they throw down their best moves and we do a battle of skateboarding talent. The adrenaline kicks in and the level of skateboarding rises. You try to blast the highest airs and the longest grinds. You try to be the best and most consistent skater in that session on that day.

We have our own music and lifestyle, which is extreme.

How do you compare skateboarding to surfing and snowboarding?

Skateboarding is similar to surfing and snowboarding. Surfing shares the fluidity of carving and turning. Snowboarding has taken from skaters all the different grabs and airs.They also share comparable physical requirements — you really have to be in shape for all of them!

Todd Huber on the lure of skating

Todd Huber is operator and part owner of SkateLab Skatepark in Simi Valley, California. This well-regarded park is where celebrities bring their kids to skate and Hollywood comes to film (Will Smith, Pamela Anderson, Gene Simmons and MTV). More importantly, Todd brings an industry insider's perspective as well as an undeniable passion for skateboarding. Todd built and maintains the world's largest skateboard museum at SkateLab. He is quoted throughout the book along with Steve Badillo.

Why do kids skate?
Kids like a *challenge*.

Take a look at ice skating. So much has been done before. If a new trick comes out in ice skating, it's like a huge deal: *Oh, he did a back flip! Oh my god, this guy did a back flip!* But most of it has pretty much been done, you know, over the last 100 years of ice skating competition.

But skateboarding is never, ever, *ever* going to be per-fected like that. There's no limit to weird stuff you can do. There's so many more tricks — it's such a young sport — maybe that's all it is — but I think in ice skating, you don't see that many different tricks in any routine. But in a skateboarding routine you can see 100 different things. I think the kids like the challenge of *not being able to perfect it.* They have no fear, and it's challenging. It's also exciting, fun and cool.

... and why it's a young person's sport

What's the age of the average skater you see?
The average age is about 14. But we've seen 'em from 3 to 16.

Is 16 getting old?
Yeah, 16. Usually about 16 they stop coming. They might come back when they're in college or get out of high school or whatever, and skate through their 20s. Or they never come back. So there's a spot, like from 16 to about 20, when they start turning into punks, get-ting into girls and cars.

But I don't think that's why it's a young person's sport. I think it's a pursuit for the young because it hurts so much when you fall — especially when you get older. With the 9-year-old kids, I see them cry once in a while,

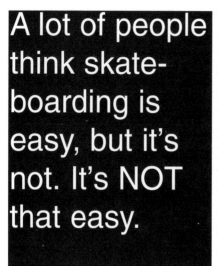

A lot of people think skateboarding is easy, but it's not. It's NOT that easy.

but for the most part, they bounce, they get up, they shake it off. The older you get, the harder it is to get up. You're not falling as hard on water or snow. Even on ice, at least you can slide it out — the energy can be transferred to your slide. But when you fall on concrete you stick, and it hurts.

I mean, my left shoulder is still sore, my wrist is still sore. I've had a lot of fun, but the older you get, you can't afford to have an injury, you can't afford to be on crutches, or not be able to use your writing hand or your computer. Because you have to go to work. Like my job, I have to be here — I have to be mobile.

... On skating dads

I can't tell you how many dads are coming back to try and learn with their kids. Even a couple of moms. We used to have a session that was for 13 years and under. But a lot of dads said *I want to go out there with Mickie, I used to skate* and they'd show up with their old board. They wanted to skate, and I had to let them in. So we called the session "Beginners Only." I thought that was pretty cool.

How do the dads do?
They try, but it's so hard, man — if you don't practice.

Do they get hurt?

Well one dad did. He came in and he thought he was going to be tough. He tried to drop in and he broke his shoulder. A lot of people think skateboarding is easy, but it's not. It's not that easy.

... On the good and bad

A lot of people think skateboarders are simply hoodlums on wheels. How about that?

There's good people and there's bad people.

Skateboarding's only 45 years old. The oldest people that did it are only in their 60s. At first it was just young people skating, but they grew up. And in growing older it seems that people got wiser — less a bunch of hoodlums or whatever.

You respect people more. I think skateboarders are normal people. They're not these extra special people,

Skate hoods hanging out.

Extreme at eighty
Here's legendary surfer, Doc Ball surfing a Tom Blake hollow
board in 1942 and then bombing the streets of Eureka,
California in 1993 (in his 80s!) Who said you couldn't ride past
25? Photos by LeRoy Grannis

and they're not criminals, either.

But there are jerks in every sport. On the negative side, I'd say that skateboarders are cheap. For example, people aren't used to paying to skateboard. SkateLab is a unique place because we have to charge people to keep the rink going. We see a lot of people that get angry because they think we're ripping them off.

But it's understandable. If they took your favorite surf break and decided to charge you $8 to surf it, you may still pay to do it, but you don't want to hear any garbage from anybody. You don't want to hear anyone telling you to put a shirt on — you just want to go and have fun. That's what we want to make sure you can do when you come here.

It been 11 years since SkateLab opened. What has changed with the beginner session?
When we started, the beginner session would get one, two, three kids, sometimes none, but now we get nine, 10 or more kids to sell out the lesson. A part of the reason for the growth in lessons is the Internet. When we first opened we had no Web site. Now our site has informed the public about our lessons, demos, contests and much more.

One way of getting beginner skaters in the SkateLab is the icebreaker event where first time skaters can get a free lesson with Steve before the park opens. It is a way for kids to get used to the park. A lot of times kids come to the SkateLab and see how jumping the ses-sions are, so the icebreaker gets the kids comfortable with the ramps and skateboarding itself.

Skateboarding is difficult. Sometimes skaters will come skate and fall and decide that they don't like it. But the icebreaker helps them see that skateboarding is fun. Then those kids will stay with skateboarding for the next five years because he or she was taught the right way with the right board.

How have you seen skate-boarding grow since SkateLab started?
It has grown overall when you look at the day we opened compared to now. It has grown, but it has gone up and down in cycles through the last 10 or 11 years.

Around 2002-2003 skateboarding was slow. That is when the icebreaker was started to get more kids introduced to skateboarding parks. There was a period when the first generation of kids that started with us grew up and moved on. The kids that were being born or were very young had to grow up to be the next generation, so there was a lag between cycles.

Helmet, elbow and knee pads are required at skate parks and **will save your butt.** If you don't believe it, check out some used gear and imagine those scrapes and gouges on your body.

Safety is
in your Head

"I think you just need to watch where you're going — that's very important — to watch what's going on around you.

But there are no terms of etiquette, like Oh, is it your turn, Charles? *or* Did you take a number? *or* Please form one line! *— it's not really like that."*

— Todd Huber / SkateLab

Safety/Courtesy: Balancing caution with aggression

Top competitors make it look easy, but it took them countless hours of relentless, calculated practice to build the confidence and expertise to perform their feats. Furthermore, they paid attention to all the rules of skateboarding safety.

It's an easy bet that without wearing the proper safety gear on their climb to the top, our top skaters wouldn't be around to impress us with their skating skills.

Safety is in your head

Know your skill level. Know what you can pull off safely. Build your expertise one skill at a time.

Protect your head, wrists, elbows and knees

Wear a helmet. Even with head protection you must be careful. If you fall on your head and feel dizzy, get a headache or experience blurry vision — you may have a concussion (brain shock). If it happens, it's very important to get medical attention right away.

Wearing long pants and long sleeved shirts helps. Better to also wear knee and elbow pads to prevent scrapes, bruises, cracked or broken bones. Wear wrist guards and sneakers with nonskid soles.

Falling

When you go down (and you will go down!) it's natural to extend your arms to break the fall. But the best way to fall is to tuck elbows in and roll on your shoulder. Kick your board away before you tumble and try to relax as you roll.

On ramps or in pools, land on your knee pads and slide. If all else fails, at least try to land on a fleshy part of your body.

Also . . .

Avoid skating in the rain. Urethane wheels slip on wet pavement.

It is wise to invest in some fitness training and to stretch before you skate.

Know how to take care of your skateboard. Make sure bolts are tight (if you can loosen with your fingers, they are not tight enough). Replace wheels when necessary. Beginners can adjust trucks so they don't wobble.

Learn new tricks one step at a time. Each trick requires a set of skills. Learn each separately before trying to put it all together. Build up to it!

At least remember this:

Avoid traffic!
Avoid tows from motor vehicles!

Caring for minor scrapes
Treat wounds immediately to avoid infection.

1. Clean with wet cloth.
2. Flush with hydrogen peroxide.
3. Dry, apply antiseptic and cover with clean bandage.
4. Each day clean with peroxide and change bandage.
5. If it doesn't begin to heal in two days, see a doctor.

What the experts say: How dangerous is skateboarding?

The U.S. Consumer Product Safety Commission states that in 2001, more than 104,000 people went to hospital emergency rooms with injuries related to skateboarding. Most had sprains, fractures, contusions and abrasions. Deaths due to collisions with cars and falling also were reported. About one in 1,000 skateboarders can expect to go to the ER with an injury.

Every year, there are about 61,000 injuries to children involving skateboards. In 2004, nearly 60,300 emergency room visits for those injuries were by children 5 to 14 years old. Six out of every 10 skateboard injuries are to children under 15 years of age.

How bad is that? Not good, of course. But studied within the context of all sports and recreational activities, there is reason to believe that skateboarding is no more risky (and in some cases less risky) than a number of other sporting and recreational pursuits.

World of Hurt

More than 30 million kids in the U.S. participate in sports each year. In fact, almost three quarters of U.S. households that have school-aged children have at least one child who plays an organized sport. It is estimated that 3.5 million children under 14 years of age receive medical treatment for sports related injuries annually.

Sports & Recreational Related Injures
Children ages 5 to 14 treated in hospital emergency rooms

Baseball/softball	116,900
Basketball	207,400
Bicycling	275,000
Football	187,800
Gymnastics	21,200
In-line skating	38,155
Skateboarding	**61,000**
Skiing/snowboarding	28,897
Soccer	76,200

Brain injury is the leading cause of sports-related death to children. Helmet use can reduce the risk of head injury by 85 percent and severe brain injury by 88 percent.

National SAFE KIDS Campaign (NSKC), *Sports Injury Fact Sheet* (Washington D.C.: NSKC, 2004).

Safe Kids Worldwide (SKW), *Bicycle, Rollerblade and Skateboard Injuries* (Washington D.C.: SKW, 2007).

Suzanne Morton, Rebecca Spicer, Alan Korn, Sue Thomas, Paul Jones, *Safe Kids U.S. Summer Safety Ranking Report* (Washington, D.C.: Safe Kids Worldwide, May 2007).

U.S. Consumer Product Safety Commission, Skateboards Publication #93.

Who, what gets hurt ...

Young children are at a greater risk of skateboarding injury than older kids due to their underdeveloped skill, strength and neuromuscular system. They are not able to sufficiently judge their own ability or traffic around them. They have a higher center of gravity, making it more difficult to protect themselves when falling. For these reasons the American Academy of Pediatrics recommends a child be at least 5 years of age before riding a skateboard.

Skateboarding accounts for about 16 percent of wheeled sport injuries to children. The three most common areas injured are the ankle, wrist and face, accounting for about 31 percent of all skateboarding related injuries. Only 5 percent of injuries are considered severe (those defined as concussions or internal injuries). But injuries such as long bone fractures or dislocations make up 31 percent of skateboard injuries. Twenty-five percent of kids that require hospitalization were hit by a motor vehicle. In 2004, an estimated 18,743 head injuries treated in emergency rooms were due to skateboarding. Deaths are rare.

American Academy of Pediatrics, Committee on Injury and Poison Prevention, *Skateboard and Scooter Injuries*, Pediatrics, Vol. 109, No. 3, March 2002.

Safe Kids Worldwide (SKW), *Bicycle, Rollerblade and Skateboard Injuries* (Washington D.C.: SKW, 2007).

... and why

- Lack of protective equipment
- Poor board maintenance
- Irregular riding surfaces
- Very young children who do not have balance or body control to prevent injury
- Riding in or near traffic

Experienced riders suffer falls after hitting rocks or irregularities in the riding surface or when they attempt difficult stunts.

Prevention

Recommendations:

1. Children under 5 years of age should not use skate boards. Their center of gravity is higher, their neuro-muscular system is not well developed, judgment is poor and they are not sufficiently able to protect themselves from injury.

2. Skateboards must never be ridden near traffic. Their use should be prohibited on streets and high-ways. Activities that bring skateboards and motor vehicles together are especially dangerous.

3. Skateboarders should be encouraged to wear helmets and protective padding for their elbows and knees to reduce or prevent injury. They should wear slip-resistant shoes.

4. Communities should be encouraged to develop safe skateboarding areas away from pedestrian and motor vehicle traffic.

American Academy of Pediatrics, Committee on Injury and Poison Prevention, *Skateboard and Scooter Injuries*, Pediatrics, Vol. 109, No. 3, March 2002.

Kids need safe places to skate! It's that simple. Get them off the street by building or letting others build better parks. Robb Field in San Diego is a great example of what can happen when public officials, the public and the skateboarding community join forces.

Tips for using a skateboard

1. Never ride in the street.
2. Don't take chances.
   - Complicated tricks require careful practice and a specially designed area.
   - Only one person per skateboard.
   - Never hitch a ride from a car or bicycle.
3. Learn how to fall.
   - If you lose balance, crouch down on the skateboard so that you will not have so far to fall.
   - In a fall, try to land on the fleshy parts of your body.
   - If you fall, try to roll rather than absorb the force with your arms.
   - Try to relax when you fall rather than stiffen.

Skateboards / Publication #93
U.S. Consumer Product Safety Commission

Steve Badillo on safety

Skateboarding can be very dangerous. If you are going to skate, you will bleed. But that's the part of skate-boarding that attracts people. The extreme aggres-sion in skating required to overcome the risk is what gives you motivation. Going fast, blasting airs and grinding long lines are what give skaters their motivation to skate for life — despite the injuries. Getting hurt is part of skateboarding.

Are there levels of skating that are less dangerous, you know, where moms and dads won't be fearful for their little kid's life?

Well, with skateboarding, nothing is safe. When you start to skateboard, you learn how to do your basic tricks, to stand on the board, to be stable, be comfortable on the board. Once you start learning more difficult tricks, you're going to fall. You may get hurt, you may bleed. So the only really safe area in skateboarding, when you're not going to get hurt, is right in the beginning, when you're just learning kickturns, carves and fakies.

And you can still fall on your butt . . .

Yeah, you can still get hurt. There's no safe technique in skateboarding that prevents falling and saves you from ever getting hurt — it's not like that.

What are the key points of safe or safer beginner skating?

Stability, balance, keeping your feet spread on the board, knowing your foot placement, knowing where you're at when you're doing the tricks, knowing your balance on the ramps and knowing transitions. Those are the things that are going to help you stay on the board and progress faster.

Would you suggest that kids wear protective gear?

Of course — knee pads, helmets, elbow pads. And I would strongly suggest wearing wrist guards. It's not necessary in a lot of the skate parks, but when you fall, you put your hands out, and the first thing that gets injured are your wrists.

Todd Huber on safety and courtesy

What are the dangers of skateboarding?

I think statistics say that the biggest dangers are irregularities in the riding surface and cars. Here in the skate park, the most common injuries are to wrists and ankles because they're the hardest things to protect. Even with protection — I've seen broken wrists with wrist guards. But I still would wear wrist guards. I swear, man, they've saved me a few times. Most people don't, though. They think it's not cool. The kids now like a kind of low-speed skating — you can usually run out any trick without having to throw it down using the pads — so it's not really a necessity until you get into speed stuff. If I was a parent, I would make my kid wear wrist guards and helmet, that's it.

That leads me to my next question. What can I do to make my skateboarding experience as safe as possible?

Well, as safe as possible. Wear knee pads, elbow pads, helmet and wrist guards. But that can be overdone. You can't skate with too much stuff on.

How about learning how to fall?

Knee pads save kids all the time — I see kids go to the knees, and that's important. When I grew up, they didn't teach how to go to the knees because there was no equipment for knees. They told you to roll but often you went to your wrist — that's why I'm so adamant about saying that wrist guards are important. But the kids now, they know to go to their knees and slide. But you'll never see a kid skating around the streets with knee pads on. You never see it because they're not going fast enough to go to the knees. It's usually on a big ramp when they step off and can't outrun it that they'll just drop and make it slide.

Is there such a thing as skateboarding courtesy or etiquette?

There's a sort of unwritten rule. You kind of have an order. Say you and your buddies are skating a ramp, you might pause longer than normal, and someone else will say *Are you gonna go?* or *I'm gonna go* or not even say that and just go. It's *almost* like you form lines — you try not to get in other people's way.

I think you just need to watch where you're going, that's very important — to watch what's going on around you.

Fortunately, you can run out most of your goofs. In fact, you'll get very, very good at it.

But there are no terms of etiquette, like *Oh is it your turn, Charles?* or *Did you take a number?* or *Time to line up!* — it's not really like that.

Just watching it's hard to see the signals.
It's a look. You just kind of look. You set up and who-ever sets up first, you just kind of make eye contact. If you don't happen to make eye contact, you might both go and you'll notice the guy and pull out — or maybe you'll both pull out — it's a little like surfing. Most of the time it's a look. You'll know who's next.

2

Skateboard/

anatomy of

"You look at the trucks, which are the metal things that hold the wheels — there's two of them. Make sure they have a name on the plate and they're not plastic. That's a dead giveaway. If they're plastic, don't buy it. And make sure there's at least some kind of a brand name on that baseplate."

—Todd Huber / SkateLab

Still Simple

After all these years, skateboards are still fairly simple. There is a board or deck to stand on, wheels to roll on and parts called trucks to steer you around.

The four major parts of a skateboard:
1. Deck
2. Trucks
3. Wheels
4. Bearings

Skaters ride on the wheels, grind on the trucks and slide on the board.

wheels go faster. Small, soft wheels are good for easy turning and quick acceleration. They're light and ideal for streetstyle. Hard wheels are good for speed and control. Vert riders like larger, harder wheels. They provide speed to perform ramp tricks.

Wheel characteristics
Diameter
Wheels range in size from 50mm to 65mm. Larger wheels are faster in racing conditions. However, smaller wheels accelerate more quickly.

Profile
This is the thickness of the wheel. The widest wheels provide the best cornering. The thinner you go, the faster you go. Thinner wheels are less stable and wear out sooner than fatter ones.

Durometer
This is the hardness of the wheel. The durometer can range from 85a to 101a. Softer wheels have a better grip on any surface and provide a smoother ride than harder wheels, but wear out faster. Harder wheels are faster on smooth surfaces.

Trucks

Trucks carry the heavy load. They serve as axles and landing gear, provide adjustable steerage and do time as a grinding surface.

They are built tough — the best are made from heat-treated aluminum. They contain steel axles to connect the wheels and steel kingpins to connect the axle to the baseplate. The baseplate is bolted to the bottom of the deck. When a rider leans to one side of his skateboard in order to turn, the trucks pivot on the kingpin in the direction of the lean.

Trucks can be adjusted to change turning speed. If the nut on the kingpin is tightened, turning will be stiffer — the board will be less wobbly. When the nut is looser, the trucks will pivot more easily — the board will turn more quickly.

Truck Parts
Kingpins
Turning the nuts on these large bolts changes the turning speed of the trucks. Note that the bolt is countersunk — it will not impede a skater's ability to grind.

Hangers
These contain the axles. Skaters grind on the hangers.

Rubber bushings
Bushings, grommets or clouds allow the trucks to pivot and turn smoothly. Different hardness of bushings will change the turning speed of the trucks. The softer your bushings are, the looser your trucks will be.

Axles
These steel rods connect the wheels.

Baseplates
Baseplates connect the trucks to the board.

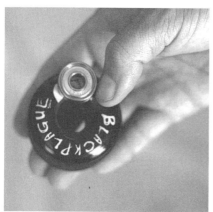

Bearings come in sealed rings that pop into either side of the wheel.

Bearings

Bearings provide spin and are located between the wheel and the axle. Bearings are assigned a special rating (called ABEC ratings) that indicate how fast they are. The higher the ABEC rating, the faster the bearing. A lower rated bearing is good for beginners.

Hardware

Bolts are used to mount the trucks and other parts to the board. You should have a skate tool (a special wrench) to adjust mounting bolts and wheels.

Clothing

Shirts. Pants. Shorts. It really doesn't matter. Fashions come and go.

Wear sneakers that aren't too bulky. They should be tough and lightweight with flat soles to better feel the board underneath.

Your first board
Borrow or rent if possible to get an idea of what you want (there's a lot to choose from). Then buy a used board.

Maintenance
Rotate wheels as you would on a car. Switch left front with right rear and right front with left rear. When you rotate, turn each wheel around as well.

Check the nuts and bolts on your trucks. If you can turn them with your fingers, they are too loose. Check the rubber bushing for wear.

Wheelbase
Wheelbase is the distance between the trucks. A short wheelbase is good for maneuverability and tricks. Longer is good for stability and speed.

Custom
Experienced riders buy trucks, wheels and board separately and put together their own skateboards.

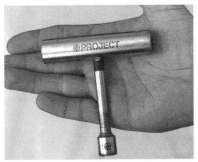

You can buy a special tool that will take care of all of your maintenance needs.

Steve Badillo on gear

How important is equipment? Are all skateboards the same?

There are many different kinds of skateboards. They all have a double kick nose and tail but the width and length vary depending on the height and weight of the individual.

What kind of skateboard should a beginner buy?

Skateboards range in width, length, concaves and wheel base. Wheels come in different hardnesses, and trucks have different turning capabilities. When you buy a skateboard, make sure to tell the dealer what type of skateboarding you do. They will help you pick the right kind of wheels, trucks and skateboard.

Can you describe the various styles of skateboards?

Differences in street boards and the most common boards are in the length, width and concave of the board itself. But you're really only dealing with a quarter inch here, a half inch there. There's not a lot of difference. Most boards are symmetrical. Some companies make really flat concaves, some really deep ones. The board I ride has a really deep concave. It gives me better foot placement, and it gives me a stronger board with a bigger pop. Some of the flatter boards are designed to flip easier.

Basically the differences in deck design include length, width and the concave of the board. Most street boards are about the same with only small variations. When you get into the longboards, then shapes change a little more. Of course, they're a lot longer and some are a little wider. The nose and the tail may look different — some are pinned and some have a square tail.

How about trucks?

It depends on the type of skating you are doing and your size. There are light trucks and heavy trucks. If you are a heavier person, you may want to get heavier trucks for grinding, so you don't break them. Those that are lighter can go with lighter trucks, so the trucks don't weigh them down. Some trucks turn really well, and there are some trucks that do not turn well at all.

Some skaters ride tight trucks, some skaters skate with loose trucks. When you skate with loose trucks, you can turn the board easily. You can also adjust yourself a little easier after landing a trick. Tight trucks are good for flipping the board, doing straight tricks and doing single tricks when you're not worrying about turning and compressing.

How about wheels?

There are lots of differences in wheels. Their sizes start at 50 millimeter all the way to 65 millimeter, which is a huge difference. They also come in different hardnesses — 92a, 95, 96, 99a, 101, 100a — the higher the number, the harder the wheel. People who skate pools normally ride a softer, bigger wheel. Those skating street are riding a smaller, harder wheel. If you're riding a variety of surfaces, you want to get something in between, maybe a 56 millimeter / 99a. The type of skateboarding you are doing, the type of terrain you're riding and how big you are will determine what kind of wheel you should be riding.

And bearings?

The bearings are fitted into the wheel itself. There are many types of bearings and a number of companies make them. Generally, the more money you pay, the faster the bearing will be.

Don't buy it! Plastic wheels, plastic mounts and the bolts are not countersunk. Boards sold by some mass merchants are junk. Always buy from a real skateboard shop.

Do you put your own bearings in your board?
Yeah.

So that's a fourth characteristic then?
Bearings are a separate entity. You fit the bearings inside the wheel. Some are fast and some are slow. The faster the bearing, the better you are going to roll. So the parts of a skateboard include the deck, trucks, wheels and bearings. There is hardware, but the hardware is basic — just bolts and nuts. It doesn't really matter — they come in different lengths, but it's no big deal.

Todd Huber on buying a skateboard

I know nothing about buying a skateboard. What do I look for?
You look at the trucks, which are the metal things that hold the wheels — there's two of them. Make sure they have some kind of a name on the plate and they're not plastic. That's a dead giveaway. If they're plastic, don't buy it. And make sure there's some kind of a brand name on the baseplate.

"Name" being the name of a company?
Yeah, Grind King, Independent, Fury, Thunder or Venture. There are probably about 10 or 12 names.

You don't want anything with the bolts sticking out — if they're not countersunk into the top, don't buy it. Every single board that's worth anything has countersunk bolts. If the whole board including the wheels and the trucks is shrink-wrapped, if the board's plastic and it's all shrink-wrapped — you see them at Venice Beach, they sell for $25 — don't buy it. I saw a Pokémon board someplace — don't buy it . . .

Pokéman? (laughing)

I'm serious, OK? If you're going to buy a brand-new board, don't spend less than $75 — no kidding — you can't even get a board at our place right now for $75.

When I buy a board, can I buy a board with everything included?

Yeah. When you don't — when you choose this board, that truck, those wheels, you pay more. But you can usually find one that's already made.

You don't have to buy the parts separately and put them together yourself?

No, no. But what I'm saying is, don't buy your board just anywhere. Don't look for a good board in a toy store — anywhere like that. Buy at a true skateboard shop — you're dumb if you don't. The imitations are from overseas. They're all plastic. The wheels are plastic. They look the same as quality wheels, but they're not. They're plastic and they're not resilient — you stick.

They're not made out of the right material . . .

The right material is urethane. And the grip — a lot of the grips are just black paint — they put it in shrink-wrap and it looks like the real deal. Parents say *Look at that! Only $39! Let's get that!*

OK, I want to buy parts and put together my own board. What's the price range for a deck?

All our decks are $50 each. We have some blanks, which are our brand name or no-name brands that are $30, but we don't push them. They're for the guy who skates a lot — like for the 14-year-old kid that skates all the time and often breaks his boards.

The blanks don't have a graphic?

Ours do, but most have something small, like a little name. Most shops have a shop board or a blank board that are a lot cheaper. But we mostly sell graphic boards at 50 bucks.

There's no performance difference . . .

There probably is. I have a feeling that the blanks aren't the same quality — if they're 20 bucks less, you know. The other thing is, if you buy blanks, you're not supporting the people who are supporting the industry with advertising and teams.

That's a big deal in skateboarding now — the blank issue?

Yeah, some people don't support the blanks. We only do it because we have a lot of kids who don't have money. They're poor kids. We have blanks for just that reason. But if you look around, our blanks are not even out — you can't even see them. The boards you see are graphic boards. You have to ask about the blanks.

How about trucks?

Some people sell cheaper ones, but our trucks range from $17.95 to $22.95 each. I figure 40 bucks for the trucks. To do it right, it's 50 bucks for your board, 40 bucks for your trucks and 30 bucks for your wheels.

Four wheels for 30 bucks?

Yeah — that's without the bearings. And the bearings cost 15 to 30 bucks. You need eight — you need two per wheel. So it's like 50 bucks for the board, 40 bucks for the trucks, that's $90, add 30 bucks for the wheels, that's $120, add 15 bucks for the bearings — that's $135. Most stores throw in grip tape for free. We do. Also bolts, which are a $7.50 savings. We do it because we're kind of new in town and want people to buy their stuff here.

So if you add it all up, it's about $135 or so?

Yeah, without tax.

For $135 plus tax you can buy the very best equipment. And in 10 minutes it will look like you beat it with a hammer.

Getting a
Feel for It

3

"Every person is different.

Some people may take a few months to learn these tricks, and others can learn them in a few days. But there are levels of skating and there are tricks — the basic tricks in skateboarding — that are easy enough for almost anyone to learn fairly quickly."

— Steve Badillo

Basics

First things

1. Before you climb onto your board, invest in quality protective gear.
2. Make sure your trucks are properly tightened and not too wobbly.
3. Find a flat, smooth, quiet area to learn. No crowds. No traffic!

Regular or goofy foot

You will stand on your board with one foot forward and one foot back. Right foot forward is called goofy foot, and left foot forward is called regular foot. There are no real reasons for the names. To discover what you are, slide across the kitchen tile in your socks. You will lead with your preferred foot. Or stand on your board both ways and see which stance feels best.

Stance

Before you put wheels to pavement, place the board on carpet or grass where it won't roll very much.

Step up on the board. Put equal weight on each foot. Feet are shoulder-width apart, placed directly over the trucks and roughly parallel to the centerline of the deck.

Assume an athletic stance. Get into a slight crouch, bend your knees and face forward. Arms are slightly raised from your sides. Relax. Feel the board beneath your feet. Practice getting on and off the board.

Keeping your upper body still and balanced over the board, slowly and carefully shift weight from toes-to-heel and heel-to-toes. This is how you steer. Feel the trucks working under your feet. Notice how you must adjust your body to stay on the board.

Pushing or kicking

Moving the board along is called pushing or kicking. Place the board on your quiet patch of pavement. Position one foot along the centerline of the deck, over or just in back of the front trucks. Push off lightly with your other foot — but don't put this foot on the board yet. Swing it forward and push off again. Practice moving and balancing on the board in this fashion, with one foot on and one foot pushing.

You may want to try this with the other foot on the board. This will help you find your most natural stance.

Practice kicking slowly across the pavement. Focus on your balance.

When you finally try placing your back foot on the board, arrange both feet so that they go across the board. Keep a wide stance, feet over the trucks, with knees slightly bent.

Stopping

What no brakes? When you bail, step off the board on the run. This should kick the board backward and prevent it from shooting out ahead and running into someone.

Chapter Three

Turning

With knees still bent, shift weight to toes to make a toeside turn and to your heels to make a heelside turn. Try making the letter S with your turns. Avoid jerky motions. Keep it smooth. Tilt the deck in the direction you wish to go. Tighten the turns by leaning into them.

Hills

Try an easy hill. Lean toward the gravity pull, just like in snowboarding or skiing. Always face downhill, top half of body pointed downhill, knees bent and arms loose. If you must stop, step off with your rear foot first. Your front foot will automatically kick the board uphill so it can be easily retrieved when it rolls back down.

Downhill control

It's easy to lose control skating straight downhill. Turning back and forth across the incline (called carving) is how to control your ride.

Remember to fall safely

You are going to fall. If you are not falling, you are not trying hard enough. If you cannot run it out . . .

1. Take the fall on your knee pads.
2. Land on flesh, not bone.
3. Try not to break falls with your hands.
4. Tuck elbows in and roll on your shoulder.

Frontside and backside

These terms come from the surfing world. Moves where a surfer faces the wave are called frontside. Moves where a surfer has his back to the wave are called backside. Likewise, when a skater faces a ramp or obstacle, it's called frontside and when he faces

away it's called backside. All moves can be done frontside and backside. A complete rider can make tricks both ways.

Frontside kickturn   Backside kickturn

Next steps

Basic tricks to learn

The next chapter gets into the following maneuvers:

1. Kickturns
2. Ollies
3. Flip tricks
4. Slides and grinds

Building tricks one skill at a time

Learn new tricks one step at a time. Each trick needs skills. Learn each separately before trying to put it all together.

Manuals and kickturns

These are important moves in developing balance. A manual is executed by riding on one set of wheels only, either front or back. A kickturn is a manual that changes direction 90, 180 or 360 degrees.

Ollies

Skaters pop Ollies to fly off the surface with the board still pressed to the bottom of their feet. This no-hands aerial is probably the most important trick in streetstyle skating.

Check it. Every airborne stunt you see in magazines or videos begins with an Ollie.

Flips

Flip tricks are like Ollies except the board is flipped or spun while airborne. Of the many types of flips, the kickflip is among the easiest to learn.

Slides and grinds

Slides are skids along a surface more or less sideways to the direction of travel. Most slides are done on the bottom of the deck. Grinds make use of the trucks. A skater skids along a surface on the hanger of his truck or trucks.

Grabs

In order to gain more control, riders often reach down and grab the deck of the skateboard during an aerial maneuver. There are numerous types of grabs.

Adjusting trucks

Turning capability can be adjusted by loosening or tightening the kingpin nut. Trucks are kept loose for the tight turning, slow-speed moves of streetstyle skating. For speed and slalom skating, trucks are tightened to help prevent shimmies.

Watch other skaters/
Hang with skaters

The possibilities for tricks are endless. Watch others and learn. Skaters may have a bad rep in general but that's fading away. Good skaters are too involved with their pursuit to use drugs and alcohol or get involved

with crime. Like athletes in any sport, they strive to stay fit, keep their mental edge and improve their skills. Many are also sensitive to the learning needs of beginners such as yourself. Chances are they will help you because, after all, other skaters helped them.

Steve Badillo on learning

So much of skating is difficult to master, but is it easy to learn some of the basics, enough to enjoy some levels of street or park skating? If so, what are those levels?

It's relatively easy to learn the basics in skateboarding, get a good feel for it and be able to skate different surfaces — parks, streets, ramps, concrete, wood — whatever. Every person is different. Some people may take a few months to learn these tricks, and others can learn them in a few days. But there are levels of skating and there are tricks — the basic tricks in skateboarding — that are easy enough for most to learn fairly quickly.

OK, what are some of the basic tricks?

Carving, Ollies, dropping in, kickturns, fakies. Once you feel comfortable with this stuff, the very next level (and it sometimes happens right away) includes grinding, axle stalls, airs and board slides. All these moves can blend during the learning process.

How long does it take to master these skills?

Depends on the individual. Like I said, for some people it may take a little longer. Some do it in just a few days.

But is there something that average kids can get their teeth into their first day — that they'll have fun with their first day?

In one day I can take a beginner and get him or her to drop in on ramps, do fakies and kickturns. I can take almost any kid and get him to do those kinds of tricks.

And that lays a nice foundation for both street and park?

That is their foundation for skateboarding — period.

The basic skills of skateboarding are all about foot placement, balance and compression. These are the basic skills that are going to help you in all of your skateboarding. When I say foot placement, I'm talking about where you put your tail foot, where you put your lead foot and how far apart your spread is for each trick. Balance is achieved by bending your knees and keeping your arms out. Compression is bending your knees and pressing down on the board while in transition, giving you thrust.

All this stuff helps you build a foundation upon which you develop basic tricks. From there you learn more advanced tricks and get creative developing your own style.

How can a skater's age affect the mental and physical challenges of learning?

When you're a little bit older the fear factor comes into play. Older riders don't want to take chances because they don't want to get hurt, obviously.

Can you be specific with ages?

Anyone past 25 usually has reservations. They won't push themselves and attempt the more difficult tricks. It's much easier for a little kid to be fearless and to try these tricks and not worry about the consequences of falling.

But if you're starting out in skateboarding a little bit older, it can still be fun. It can be totally fun — you can take it a little bit slower and still learn all the basics. I have a friend who is 26 years old who's just starting to skate and he's progressing really well. So it's really up to the individual. Skateboarding is so much an individual sport. It's up to each person what he wants to get out of it. It can be more difficult for people who are older, but it's not impossible. They can have creativity with it, they can have fun with it, and they can progress in it.

Skateboarding is a mental thing, isn't it?

It's definitely a mental thing. You can be taught how to do the trick, but what it takes to actually land that trick is commitment, telling yourself you can make it and visualizing yourself doing it.

Right from the beginning . . .

Right from the beginning — even when you're doing the most basic tricks — you have to commit yourself to pulling that trick. If you don't see yourself pulling that trick — if you don't commit — you will fall.

So when you learn new stuff you have to commit yourself, see yourself doing it and be confident in yourself. Because in the beginning all the tricks seem gnarly — even the small ones.

When you learn
new stuff you
have to commit
yourself, see
yourself doing it
and be confi-
dent in yourself.

Years of dedicated practice go into a move like this.
Steve makes it look easy (yeah, he made it!).

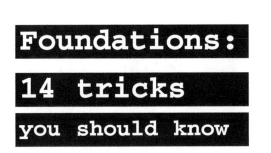

Foundations:
14 tricks
you should know

4

"It's definitely a mental thing.
You can be taught how to do the trick, but what it takes to actually land that trick is commitment, telling yourself you can make it and visualizing yourself doing it."

— Steve Badillo

Build/blend

This chapter is full of instructional footage. There are lots of ways to learn, but studying what we have thrown down here is a very good way to begin.

You may want to try this stuff in the order it's presented since the tricks build upon each other. You will find that the maneuvers overlap and that after skating for a while, they blend and lead to other things. That's because skateboarding is not a structured pursuit and is bound only by a rider's imagination.

"The basic skills of skateboarding are all about foot placement, balance and compression.

These are things that are going to help you in all of your skateboarding.

When I say foot placement, I'm talking about where you put your tail foot, where you put your lead foot and how far apart your spread is for each trick.

Balance is achieved by bending your knees and keeping your arms out.

Compression is bending your knees and pressing down on the board while in transition, giving you thrust.

All this stuff helps you build a foundation upon which you develop basic tricks. From there you learn more advanced tricks and get creative developing your own style."

— Steve Badillo

Patterns

When you analyze the sequences that follow, it may be helpful to note the similar actions and patterns. For example, every skating trick involves compression — the extension (unweighting) and compression (weighting) of your body to gain speed or pop yourself up into the air ...

Every time you go up or down an incline or transition there is a specific way to weight your-self on the board — especially when you're going down (lean into the drop — or else) ...

And just about every time you leave the earth you will be executing an Ollie ...

Everything connects and draws from something else. It's not so much knowing the tricks as it is understanding the underlying dynamics of how a skater suc-cessfully rides a skateboard up, down and over things. Practicing the tricks will defi-nitely get you in touch with that.

Then it's all up to you.

Solid spread

Foot placement

For the most part, skaters ride with feet well spread, planted over the bolts and parallel to each other. To perform certain tricks, like Ollies and kickflips, placement is initially altered, as illustrated on the next page. As shown below, you can simulate dropping in on a flat surface before you try a ramp.

Dropping in

Ollie

Kickflip

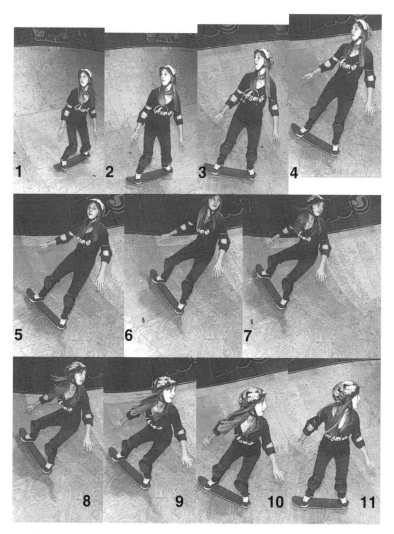

Compressions / forward and fakie

Compression creates speed. As you go up the transition (or incline), straighten your knees (extend) and keep your arms out for balance. As you go down, bend at the hips and knees and push down on your board (compress) and lean into the new direction.

Build speed by executing more compressions. Assuming you started the run going forward, coming back down you will be riding fakie or backward (you really should learn to ride backward as well as forward). The mechanics of compression are the same.

Carving in a bowl / compression in action

Jack rides around and up and down the sides of the bowl utilizing gravity pull and compression to accelerate. Note the extension in photos #1, #2, #10, #11, #12, #21 and #22. Each is followed by compression in photos #4, #5, #6, #14 and #15.

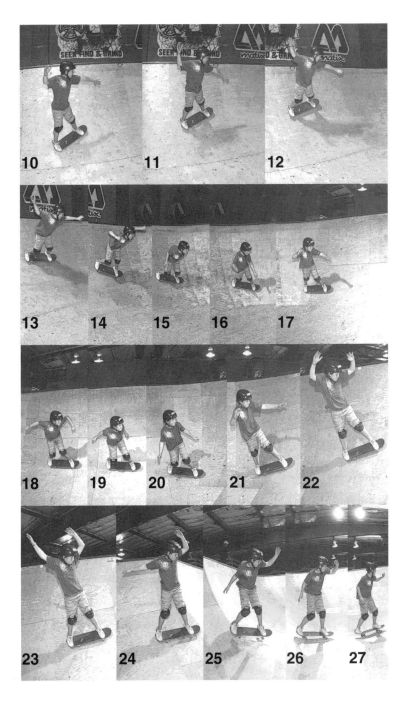

Frontside kickturn

Called frontside because the skater is facing the ramp or transition during the turn. Riley extends as he rides up the ramp and pushes down on the tail when he starts his turn. Be sure to turn your head and shoulders as you swing the board around 180 degrees and back down, bending at the hips and leaning forward.

Backside kickturn

4

Your back faces the ramp during the turn, hence the name. As you go up the transition, push down on the tail and turn the nose of the board 180 degrees. The turn is made by rotating your head and shoulders and pressing your weight forward down the incline. Riley extends on the way up and compresses as he rides downhill, pushing down on his board to accelerate.

Dropping in

Gavin positions the tail of his board on the coping (usually the metal edge of the ramp or bowl) so that the back wheels are on the downhill side of the coping. Place your front foot on the top of the bolts. Feet must be parallel. When you drop in, press straight down the ramp with all your weight and lean forward with your head. To help you lean forward, try grabbing the nose of your board. Compress at the bottom transition for additional speed.

Ollie

This is the most fundamental trick in skateboarding. Alex's back foot is on the tail and his front foot is in the middle of the board. From a compressed position, he at once jumps up, snaps the tail on the ground and pulls his front foot toward the nose. His front foot levels out the board in flight. Land with your feet spread on the board. An Ollie is difficult to master and you will spend countless hours perfecting it.

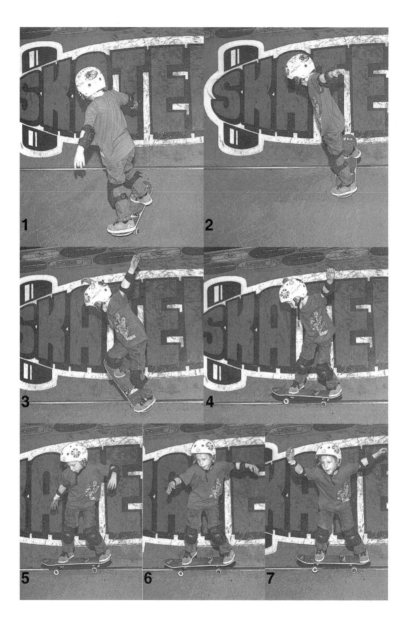

Axle stall

Patrick's feet are parallel and spread on the board. Ride up the transition to the coping. Lock your back truck on the coping, turn backside and lay your front truck on the coping. To descend, push down on your tail and lift the nose up and around 90 degrees. Lean forward, drop back down the ramp and ride it out.

Backside 50/50 grind

Feet are spread and parallel. Gage rides up the transition with good speed. Carve up at an angle and place the back truck over the coping. Lean forward, center your weight over the board, place the front truck over the coping and grind. When you want to come back down, lean toward the flat bottom, push down on the tail and bring yourself around 90 degrees. Weight must be forward as you descend.

Rock n roll fakie

Feet are spread and parallel on the board. Ride up the transition and lap your front truck over the coping onto the top deck, keeping the nose of the board straight. See Devin quickly turn his head fakie (but not his shoulders) toward the flat bottom. Press down on the tail (which leads the way down) and lean into the ramp back down (which is fakie — so you must be confident riding backward).

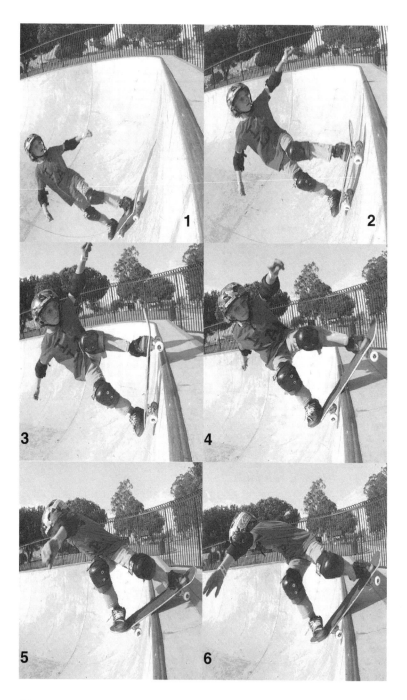

Rock n roll

Do this like a kickturn, but on the coping. Keep your feet spread and parallel on the board. Jackson travels up the transition and rolls his front truck over the coping onto the top deck, keeping the nose of the board straight. Immediately turn your head and shoulders toward the flat bottom. Press down on the tail, bring the nose around 180 degrees, lean forward and ride it out.

Boardslide

Note that an Ollie gets Michael up and on the rail. Aim for the center of the board to slide on the rail. With your feet spread and your balance leaning down the rail you will slide through. At the end of the rail swing the nose of the board around 90 degrees, land on your wheels and ride away. There are backside boardslides (like this) as well as frontside, noseslides and tailslides.

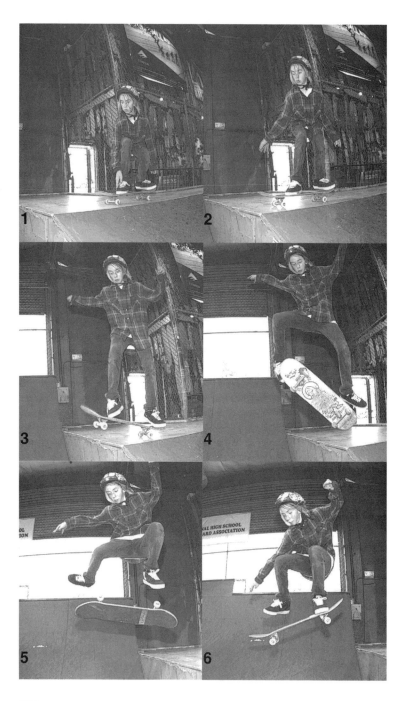

Kickflip

You must know how to do Ollies. Position your back foot on the tail and your front foot in the middle of the board on your heelside edge. Snap the tail for the Ollie and at the same time lift your front foot toward the nose, pressing down and out. This will flip your board. Lift your knees so that the board can flip freely. Notice how Zach lands on the board with feet spread over the bolts.

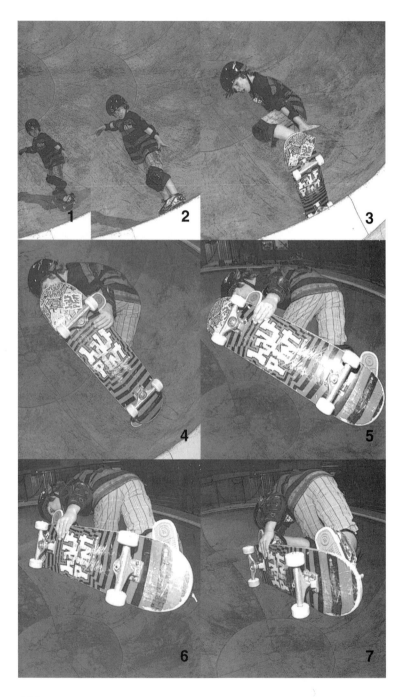

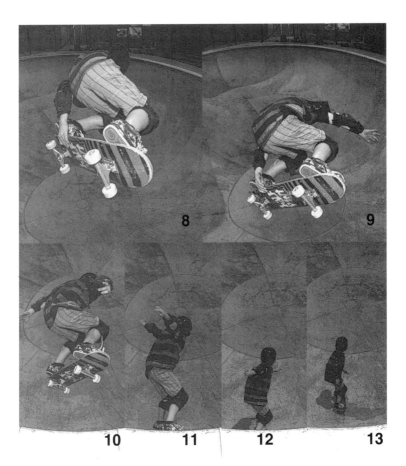

Backside air

Airs come in all shapes and sizes. Backside airs require that you feel comfortable executing backside Ollies. Ride up to the transition with a lot of speed (the faster you go, the higher the air). When you reach the coping, blast an Ollie and reach down with your lead hand and grab the deck behind your front wheel. In the air, turn your head and shoulders and the nose of the board 180 degrees back toward the transition. Tom lets go of the board just before landing. Remember to lean forward when you descend the transition.

Manual

Manuals have many different variations. Steve is doing an Ollie into the manual. The faster you go, the longer you can hold the manual position. Lean back, center over your back truck and lift the nose of the board. Keep your arms out for balance. Try not to skid your tail while holding the manual. When you lose speed or balance, put the nose of the board down and try again.

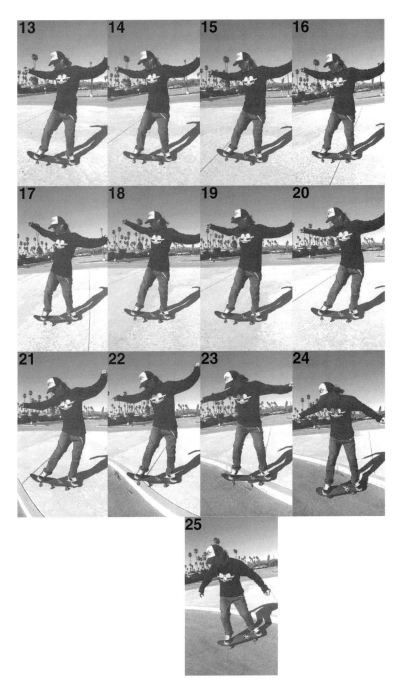

The early years of skateboarding were somewhat faddish, whimsical and just plain off-the-wall. Robin and John Finlayson share a moment on a motorized skateboard in 1964. Photo by LeRoy Grannis

Scooter wheels circa 1933. We have come a long, long way.

"The Ollie — just like the cockroach
— kept getting perfected and bigger and used more technically and now it's universal. There are a million tricks that have progressed from one Ollie."

— Todd Huber / SkateLab

A history:
Boom! Bust! Boom!

Scooters and roller skate wheels

The first skateboardlike vehicle dates to the early 1900s. This was a homemade scooter made from metal roller skate wheels and two by fours. Scooters had waist-high handles at first but in time the handles were discarded to leave only a plank with the steel wheels. This was skateboarding for about 50 years.

Sidewalk surfing

The first commercial skateboards were sold in 1959. This coincided with surfing's first burst of popularity and there was a tie between the two sports. Surfers skated when the waves were poor and developed early riding technique. The phrase "sidewalk surfing" was born and stuck in people's minds. Surfboard manufacturers, notably Hobie Alter, produced skateboards and promoted skateboarding through hugely successful tours and demonstrations.

Magazines and popular music fanned the flames. Skateboarding fast caught the imagination of a faddish, teen-aged nation and boomed in the early '60s. It is estimated that more than 50 million boards were sold in a three-year period.

Skateboarding in the '60s was downhill racing, carving, slalom and various acrobatics such as handstands and jumps. Boards were flat and wheels were made of clay. Wheels and trucks came from a roller skate manufacturer in Chicago.
Photo by LeRoy Grannis

During this first short-lived era, steel wheels gave way to smoother riding clay wheels. The trucking devices that attach wheels to the riding platform were improved (somewhat) also. Clay wheels, however, did not grip riding surfaces and were partially to blame for numerous skateboarding accidents.

> **Trouble from the start**
> The May 1965 cover of *Life* magazine featured Pat McGee, National Girls' Champion doing a handstand. The photo was captioned: *The Craze and the Menace of Skateboards.*
>
> **And about the same time . . .**
> The California Medical Association reported that skateboarding was nearly as dangerous as bicycle riding.

Meanwhile, John Q. Public mostly viewed the new sport as intrusive and dangerous. When kids began suffering major injuries from their falls, cities began to wipe the sport from the streets. The first skateboarding boom disappeared in the fall of 1965 when orders for skateboards came to a crashing halt. Unsold inventory resulted in large losses for manufacturers. It would take eight years for the sport to revive.

Birth of vertical riding
In the mid-'60s riders began skating in empty pools. Since the direction of their efforts was largely up and down, this came to be known as vertical skating. Although practiced only by the brave few, this was a significant departure from what riding had been — downhill racing, carving, slalom and various acrobatics

such as handstands and jumps. Pool riding was the genesis of the hard-riding, airborne, alpha-athletic performances today's public has come to associate with the sport.

Because they rode on traction-challenged clay wheels these pioneers could not skate beyond the coping (pool's edge) like today's expert riders. The hot bed of pool activity in the '60s was Santa Monica, California (a.k.a. Dogtown).

Rebirth in 1973

Technological breakthroughs gave rise to the second coming of skateboarding. In 1973 the first set of urethane wheels were sold. Urethane is a petroleum-based product that was developed in Germany in the 1930s. Urethane better gripped the riding surface enabling riders to skate more acrobatically. Precision-bearing wheels and better trucks further enhanced performance. Skate publications captured the mind boggling maneuvers by the era's top riders and spread the spirit of a new skateboarding movement. Skateboard manufacturing flourished and once again tours and contests turned on youthful onlookers.

In 1976 the first outdoor skateboard park opened in Florida, and soon hundreds were built across the United States. Parks encouraged vertical riding and forever changed the scope and style of skateboarders who were increasingly eager to push limits.

Pool riding became hot, and with the aid of the new technology, skaters were able to skate up and finally over the coping. The concept of air — flying on a

skateboard — was born. Riders took their vertical moves from the parks to the streets and developed that particularly unfettered and fearless genre of skateboarding known as streetstyle.

In the late '70s Alan "Ollie" Gelfand provided one of the single greatest breakthroughs in skating performance. After hours of practice in an abandoned Florida pool, he devised and perfected a way to flip a skateboard into the air with his rear foot while keeping the front foot (as well as the rear foot) on the board. The Ollie is literally how a skater flies through space with a board seemingly glued to his feet. The magical no-hands aerial is a cornerstone of modern skating.

Wheels made all the difference — From bottom to top — metal wheels jarred bones and clay wheels could not grip, but urethane wheels paved the way for high performance.

It was during this period that skateboarding's unique culture and brotherhood further developed. The sport became increasingly aggressive in performance and style. Skaters identified with raw, cutting edge music and created their own graphic look. The bottoms of their boards became showcases for the latest hot visual.

Alan "Ollie" Gelfand invented the most important trick in modern skateboarding with the no-hands aerial in the late '70s. The creation of the Ollie and the introduction of urethane skateboard wheels in 1973 are widely considered to be the most significant events in skate history.

But by 1980 issues of safety once again stifled popular growth. Skateboarding parks could not afford rocketing insurance costs and shut down. Skateboarding went underground. Hardcore riders kept the sport alive by riding backyard ramps and halfpipes and by taking it to the streets.

In 1981 the first issue of *Thrasher* magazine was published. *Thrasher* was and still is dedicated to the hardcore skater. As the sport struggled in the early '80s, the magazine provided a valuable focus for the skateboarding community. *Thrasher* also promoted the latest musical trends and encouraged an underground mentality that included a disdain for the mainstream and a totally fearless obsession to skate on any surface, anywhere. This philosophy came to be known as "skate and destroy."

Back Again in 1983

Another boom began in 1983. Vertical riding, streetstyle and freestyle skating all became popular and each boasted expert riders that starred in skateboarding magazines and videos. Videos, in particular, promoted and encouraged the '80s skateboarding boom.

Transworld Skateboarding magazine was founded in 1984 and has become one of skating's more powerful influences. *Transworld* promoted and still promotes skateboarding through top notch photography and graphics as well as through a broad, inclusive philosophy. In other words, parents of young skaters could read it and not be offended or frightened that skateboarding would steal little Johnny's (or Suzie's) soul.

For the first time, significant money could be made by a pro skater through product endorsements and contests. Top riders could conceivably ride for a living.

Certain manufacturers prospered. Skateboarding developed its own fashions. Skateboarding shoes in particular caught on with mainstream buyers. As the decade wore on, top riders broke off from the larger manufacturers and started their own companies and labels.

By the late '80s streetstyle dominated and vertical riding became less popular. The recession of the early '90s marked the end of the third boom.

Skating into the future

Issues that once held the popularity of skateboarding in check have either been dealt with or do not appear on the horizon today.

1. Superior equipment has paved the way for greater performance.

2. Amended Health and Safety Codes have resulted in a resurgence of park development nationwide.

3. Safety is always a concern, but studies show that skateboarding is less dangerous than once was thought (safer than football, in-line skating and hockey — based on percentage of participants injured).

4. Even in our struggling economy, the business of skateboarding is doing very well. This translates into an expanded insurgence of tours, videos, contests, promotions and exposure for all kids.

5. Skateboarding has a history. After all these years, mainstream America considers skateboarding a real sport — something to watch on TV with the family.

6. YouTube and the Internet have made a profound impact on the sport of skateboarding. Now, any skater can make a video of himself doing his best tricks and broadcast it on the Web for the world to see. No longer do we need to wait anxiously by the mailbox for the latest skate magazine. We can get information about the best pros, parks and products with the click of a mouse.

All this means skateboarding actually has a future. The sport is finally here to stay. Believe it.

Back for good

Skateboarding's icons have solidified the sport's place in mainstream culture. Danny Way continues to push the envelope, traveling the world and setting amazing records. Paul Rodriguez, Jr., the current face of the sport, is winning big contests and getting big endorsements from the likes of Nike. Rob Dyrdek and Ryan Sheckler are living the life on their hit MTV shows. Bam Margera and his *Jackass* crew have invaded our planet with shows, movies and insane skateboard stunts. Hollywood has even brought skateboarding to the silver screen, introducing a whole new generation to the roots of skating in the *Lords of Dogtown*. Tony Hawk ... the guy is everywhere and rubs elbows with the most elite athletes on earth.

Skate fashions (again, especially shoes) are hot items with skaters and non-skaters alike. The major skating style and trend continues to be streetstyle.

Landmark Legislation

In 1997 California's Health and Safety Code was amended to legally classify skateboarding as a hazardous activity. This means skateboarders assume the risks of their pursuit and cannot sue if they are injured while skating in a public facility. Developers were no longer yoked by liability and began building parks once more. This change in California's code has encouraged other states to do the same. As a result there are more than 300 parks nationwide with more on the way.

Todd Huber on skating's greatest museum

How about this museum? This is a lifetime thing for you, isn't it?

Not really. It came about when I quit smoking. The person that helped me quit said to figure out how much money I would normally spend on cigarettes and use that money, energy and time to do something useful. So I got into collecting skateboards.

How many years?

Since 1991 we have collected more than 5,000 skateboards. We still go out looking, we get some on the Internet and people bring in donations. This is the largest skateboard museum in the world.

SkateLab is recognized by the state — we have a plaque on the wall I'm pretty proud of. We are, in fact, protecting one of California's historical resources. Skateboarding is something that got started here in California.

Skateboarding was born around here, right?
Yeah, in the San Fernando Valley. The first skateboard shop was Val's Surf and it's still owned by Mark Richards, who's one of the guys instrumental in developing the first skateboard introduced to the marketplace. Up to that point skateboards were made out of a piece of wood with roller skate wheels nailed onto it.

Mark Richards called the Chicago Roller Skate Company and got them to send the front halves of their roller skates and attached them to surfboard-style boards — there's a couple of them here. He and Hobie Alter made a couple models. He had the the very first skate shop — it's like only 20 minutes from here. Mark has donated a lot of cool stuff to the museum. There are some bitchin' pictures of him by LeRoy Grannis — taken a week after I was born. He'd be steamed if he heard about that. Like in the same year I was born, there are pictures of him skateboarding. That's what I like about the sport — it started here.

How is this museum recognized by the state?

We're a member of the California State Historical Society. We're on the list of museums in California, which is a difficult thing to accomplish. It's serious. People come to SkateLab just to look at the museum. We have so much stuff. Pro stuff, toys, games, patents, uniforms, records, helmets, scooters, shoes, wheels — we have everything.

What's the most interesting to you?

Some dad brought in this unusual board called the Skate Wing from Australia — you can probably get a picture of it — it's hanging right above the counter and it's like a skateboard with wings and an extra wheel is attached to each.

Wheels on the wings? (laughing)

It's pretty funny. One of the kids that skates here said *Oh, I wanna try it — I want to be the guy!* He got up on the highest ramp and everybody was watching him. There's was a line all the way down the hall — probably about 30 people waiting to get in. So he dropped it off the top of the ramp, lost control and hit the edge of that thing and it doubled him over. I felt sorry for him — but he didn't get hurt — just a bruise on the wrist.

First wheelies and kickturns — Flat, rigid boards, roller skate trucks and clay wheels made for limited performance in 1965. Mark Richards is the skater.
Photos by LeRoy Grannis

Mark Richards was one of the first manufacturers of skateboards. In the '60s he shaped the decks to look like surfboards and attached roller skate trucks and wheels. His company, Val Surf, was the first skateboard shop and it still thrives in the San Fernando Valley just outside of Los Angeles.

Boardslides from the year 2009 (Steve Badillo) and 1965 (Mark Richards). In 45 years skateboarding has grown from a lark to a major sport and leisure activity across the globe.
Photo of Mark Richards by LeRoy Grannis

Riding the nose of a skateboard (to emulate the surfing maneuver) was a pretty big deal in the early days.
Photo by LeRoy Grannis

Glossary

Air: When a skater leaves the riding surface with his skateboard.

Axle Stall: When a rider skates up a transition, momentarily rests his board on its trucks (hangers) on the coping, and rides back down.

Backside: A move or position where a skater has his or her back turned to the obstacle.

Baseplate: That part of the truck that attaches to the deck.

Blank: Refers to a skate deck that has no graphic art.

Carving: When a skater turns back and forth over a riding surface — usually to control a downhill ride.

Compression: When a skater compresses (pushes down) and extends his or her body in order to accelerate.

Concave: Refers to the scooped, dishlike quality of a molded skateboard deck.

Coping: The metal edge located at the top of ramps and pools.

Deck: The riding platform of a skateboard. Also called the board.

Dropping In: When a skater descends a ramp from a still position.

Durometer: Refers to the hardness of a skate wheel.

Fakie: Riding backward.

Fliptrick: Refers to any number of tricks where the skateboard is flipped or spun underneath the feet.

Freestyle: Usually refers to tricks performed on a flat riding surface.

Frontside: A move where a skater faces the obstacle.

Goofy Foot: Right foot forward.

Grab: When a rider reaches down and grabs the deck of the skateboard during an aerial maneuver.

Grind: When a skater rides the trucks of his skateboard — specifically the hangers.

50/50 Grind: When a rider skates up a transition, places both trucks (hangers) on the coping and rides along the coping in this fashion for a distance.

Grip Tape: The self-adhesive, sandpaperlike covering that is applied to the deck of a skateboard.

Hanger: That part of a truck that contains the axle and connects the wheels. Skaters ride or grind on the hangers.

Hardware: Refers to the mounting bolts that attach the trucks to the deck.

Kick: Refers to the molded upturn of the nose and deck of a skate deck.

Kickflip: When a rider flips the skateboard underneath his or her feet and lands back on the deck.

Kicking: Standing and pushing along on a skateboard.

Kingpin: That part of a truck that connects the hanger and axle to the baseplate. This bolt adjusts turning capability.

Kickturn: When a skater pivots on one set of wheels and changes direction.

Longboards: Usually refers to skateboards more than 35 inches in length.

Ollie: When a skater snaps a skateboard into the air, levels it out and controls the flight with his or her feet only.

Profile: Refers to the thickness of a skate wheel.

Regular Foot: Left foot forward.

Rock n Roll Fakie: When a rider skates up a transition, rolls one set of wheels over the coping (so that the rider is resting the bottom of the board on the coping), leans back down the transition and rides it out going backward or fakie.

Rock n Roll: When a rider skates up a transition, rolls one set of wheels over the coping (so that the rider is resting the bottom of the board on the coping), turns board and body 180 degrees and rides back down the transition.

Skate and Destroy: The hardcore streetskaters creed: Ride (upon and over) anything, anytime.

Skate, Skaters, Skating: An abbreviated way to say skateboard (verb), skateboarders, skateboarding.

Skate park: A public or private skating area that contains various skateable terrains.

Slide: The act of riding or sliding along a riding surface using the deck (usually the bottom) of a skateboard. Also boardslide.

Streetstyle: Refers to the type of riding required to skate obstacles in the streets like curbs, handrails and benches.

Transition: Refers to any incline rising from a flat riding surface.

Trucks: The metal apparatus that connects the wheels

to the deck of a skateboard. Trucks provide steerage and serve as landing gear.

Urethane: The special plasticlike material that skateboard wheels are made of.

Vert: Vertical. Refers to ramp riding — especially on steeper, higher ramps.

Wheelbase: The distance between the two trucks on a skateboard.
Wheelie: When a skater balances upon one set of wheels.

Bibliography

American Academy of Pediatrics, Committee on Injury and Poison Prevention, *Skateboard and Scooter Injuries*, Pediatrics, Vol. 109, No. 3, March 2002.

http://www.signonsandiego.com/news/business/20041005-9999-1b5alva.html, *Chairman of his boards: Skating icon uses hands-on approach with business.*

National SAFE KIDS Campaign (NSKC), *Sports Injury Fact Sheet* (Washington D.C.: NSKC, 2004).

Safe Kids Worldwide (SKW). *Bicycle, Rollerblade and Skateboard Injuries* (Washington D.C.: SKW, 2007).

Safe Kids Worldwide (SKW). *Childhood Injury Trends Fact Sheet* (Washington D.C.: SKW, 2007).

Suzanne Morton, Rebecca Spicer, Alan Korn, Sue Thomas, Paul Jones, *Safe Kids U.S. Summer Safety Ranking Report* (Washington, D.C.: Safe Kids Worldwide, May 2007).

U.S. Consumer Product Safety Commission, Skateboards Publication #93.

Wallis AL, Cody BE, Mickalide AD, *Report to the Nation: Trends in Unintentional Childhood Injury Mortality, 1987-2000* (Washington D.C.: National SAFE KIDS Campaign, May 2003).

Resources

Here we have a healthy dose of info about skateboarding as it relates to:

Books
Camps
Magazines
Museums
Organizations
Professional skateboarding events
Shops
Skateparks
Skatepark designers
Videos
Web sites

For a quick fix go to **skateboarding.com** This is an informative (but not the only) portal into the skateboarding galaxy. For face-to-face, find a skateboard shop and talk to skaters.

Books

Books discovered on Amazon.com and Barnesandnoble.com

Baccigaluppi, John. *Declaration of Independents.* San Francisco, California: Chronicle Books, 2001.

Bermudez, Ben. *Skate! The Mongo's Guide to Skateboarding.* New York, New York: Cheapskate Press, 2001.

Borden, Ian. *Skateboarding, Space and the City.* New York, New York: Berg, 2001.

Brooke, Michael. *The Concrete Wave: The History of Skateboarding.* Toronto, Ontario: Warwick Publishing, 1999.

Burke, L.M. *Skateboarding! Surf the Pavement.* New York, New York: Rosen Publishing Group, Inc., 1999.

Cliver, Sean. *Disposable: A History of Skateboarding Art.* Thornhill, Ontario: Concrete Wave Editions, 2004.

Davis, James. *Skateboard Roadmap.* England: Carlton Books Limited, 1999.

Gould, Marilyn. *Skateboarding.* Mankato, Minnesota: Capstone Press, 1991.

Gutman, Bill. *Skateboarding: To the Extreme.* New York, New York: Tom Doherty Associates, Inc., 1997.

Hardwicke, Catherine. *Lords of Dogtown.* Thornhill, Ontario, Canada: Concrete Wave Editions, 2005.

Hawk, Tony. *Hawk Occupation: Skateboarder.* New York, New York: Regan Books, 2001.

Mullen, Rodney. *The Mutt: How to Skateboard and not Kill Yourself.* New York, New York: Regan Books, 2004.

Powell, Ben. *Extreme Sports: Skateboarding.* Hauppauge, New York: Barron's Educational Series, Inc., 1999.

Riggins, Edward. *Ramp Plans.* San Francisco, California: High Speed Productions, 2000.

Ryan, Pat. *Extreme Skateboarding.* Mankato, Minnesota: Capstone Press, 1998.

Shoemaker, Joel. *Skateboarding Streetstyle.* Mankato, Minnesota: Capstone Press.

Thrasher. *Insane Terrain.* New York, New York: Universe Publishing, 2001.

Camps

IPS
School of Skate
PO Box 1530
Hood River, Oregon 97031
School_of_skate@sk8ips.com

Lake Owen
HC 60 Box 60
Cable, Wisconsin 54821
715-798-3785

Magdalena Ecke Family YMCA
200 Saxony Road
Encinitas, California 92023-0907
760-942-9622

Mission Valley YMCA
5505 Friars Road
San Diego, California 92110
619-298-3576

SkateLab
Atlantic Beach Skatecamp
16 W. 3rd St.
Atlantic Beach, Florida 32233
904-249-2529
skatelab.com

SkateLab
Steve Badillo Skate Camp
4226 Valley Fair St.
Simi Valley, California 93063
805-578-0040
skatelab.com

Snow Valley
PO Box 2337
Running Springs, California 92382
909-867-2751

Visalia YMCA
Sequoia Lake, CA
211 West Tulare Avenue
Visalia, California 93277
559-627-0700

Woodward Camp
PO Box 93
132 Sports Camp Drive
Woodward, Pennsylvania 16882
814-349-5633

Woodward Lake Owen
46445 Krafts Point Road
Cable, Wisconsin 54821
715-798-3785

Woodward West
28400 Stallion Springs Road
Tehachapi, California 93561
661-882-7900

Young Life Skate Camp
Hope, British Columbia, Canada
604-807-3718

Magazines

Juice
4090 Valley Meadow Road
Encino, California 91436
310-399-5336
juicemagazine.com

Thrasher
High Speed Productions
1303 Underwood Avenue
San Francisco, California 94124
415-822-3083
thrashermagazine.com

Skateboarder
Surfer Publications
PO Box 1028
Dana Point, California 92629
skateboardermag.com

Transworld Skateboarding
353 Airport Road
Oceanside, California 92054
760-722-7777
skateboarding.com

Museums

Board Gallery
Newport Beach, California

Huntington Beach International Skate
and Surf Museum
411 Olive St.
Huntington Beach, California
714-960-3483

SkateLab
4226 Valley Fair St.
Simi Valley, California 93063
805-578-0040
skatelab.com

Skatopia
34961 Hutton Rd.
Rutland, Ohio 45775
740-742-1110

Organizations

Action Sports Retailer
Organizer of the Action Sports Retailer
Trade Expos.
949-376-8144
asrbiz.com

C.A.S.L. and P.S.L.
California Amateur Skateboard League
Professional Skateboard League
Amateur and professional contest
organizer.
909-883-6176
Fax 909-883-8036

Extreme Downhill International
1666 Garnet Ave. #308
San Diego, California 92109
619-272-3095

International Association of
Skateboard Companies
PO Box 37
Santa Barbara, California 93116
805-683-5676
iascsk8@aol.com
skateboardiasc.org

International Network for Flatland
Freestyle Skateboarding
Abbedissavagen 15
746 95 Balsta, Sweden

KC Projects
Canadian amateur contest organizer.
514-806-7838
kc_projects@aol.com
5148067838@fido.ca

National Amateur Skateboard
Championships
Damn Am Series
National amateur contest organizer.
813-621-6793
skateparkoftampa.com
nascseries.com

N.H.S.S.A.
National High School Skateboard
Association
jeffreystern@roadrunner.com
805-990-4209

National Skateboarders Association of
Australia (NSAA)
Amateur and professional contest
organizer.
61-2-9878-3876
skateboard.asn.au

The Next Cup
Southern California amateur contest
organizer.
858-874-4970 Ext. 114 or 129
thenextcup.com

Skateboarding Association of America
Amateur contest organizer.
727-523-0875
skateboardassn.org

Skatepark Association of the USA
(SPAUSA)
Resource for skatepark planning /
operating.
310-823-9228
spausa.org

Southwest Sizzler
Southwestern amateur contest
organizer.
918-638-6492

Surf Expo
East Coast trade show.
800-947-SURF
surfexpo.com

Supergirl
beasupergirl.com

United Skateboarding Association
(USA)
Skate event organizer and action sport
marketing / promotions.
732-432-5400 Ext. 2168 and 2169
unitedskate.com

Vans Shoes
Organizer of the Triple Crown skate
events.
562-565-8267
vans.com

World Cup Skateboarding
Organizer of some of skating's largest
events.
530-888-0296
Danielle@wcsk8.com
wcsk8.com

Zeal Skateboarding Association
Southern California amateur contest
organizer.
909-265-3420
zealsk8.com

Professional skateboarding events

All Girl Skate Jam
myspace.com
(Search for All Girl Skate Jam)

Gravity Games H2O
Gravitygamesh20.com

Tony Hawk's Boom Boom Huck Jam
boomboomhuckjam.com

Mountain Dew Tour
astdewtour.com

Vans Triple Crown of Skateboarding
vans.com/vans/events

Warped Tour
vans.com/vans/events

X Games
Expn.go.com/expn

Shops and companies

Black Plague Wheels
85 Mahogany Lane
Simi Valley, CA 93065
818-439-2683
blackplaguewheels.com

IPS Skateboards
IPS Skate & Snow Shop
13 Oak Street
Hood River, Oregon 97031
541-386-6466
sk8ips.com
wally@sk8ips.com
skateshop@sk8ips.com

Santa Monica Airlines Skateboards
3435 Ocean Park Blvd. #107/151
Santa Monica, CA 90405
www.smaskateboards.com

Skateboarding.com

Skateboards.org

SkateLab
4226 Valley Fair St.
Simi Valley, California 93063
805-578-0040
skatelab.com

Steadham Skate Ind.
stevesteadham.com
myspace.com/stevesteadham
stevesteadham@hotmail.com
ssteadham@gmail.com
702-416-8331

Tailtap
PO Box 1895
Carlsbad, California 92018
tailtap.com

Skateparks

Bear Creek Skatepark
625 Highland Drive
Medford, Oregon

Burnside Projects
Underneath the east side of the
Burnside Bridge
Portland, Oregon

Camarillo Skateboard Park
1030 Temple Avenue
Camarillo, California

Chehalem Skate Park
1201 Blaine Street
Newberg, Oregon

Culver City Skateboard Park
Jefferson Blvd. and Duquesne Ave.
Culver City, California

Brian Haney Memorial Skatepark
Main Street and 13th Street
Aumsville, Oregon

Lincoln City Skatepark
NE Reef Street
Lincoln, City, Oregon

Montclair Skatepark
5111 Benito Street
Montclair, California

Oxnard Skateboard Park
3250 South Rose Avenue
Oxnard, California

Pedlow Skate Park
17334 Victory Boulevard
Encino, California

Skateboarding.com

Skateboards.org

SkateLab
4226 Valley Fair St.
Simi Valley, California 93063
805-578-0040
skatelab.com

Ken Wormhoudt Skate Park
225 San Lorenzo Boulevard
Santa Cruz, California

Skatepark designers

Airspeed Skateparks LLC
2006 Highway 101 #154
Florence, Oregon 97439
503-791-4674
airspeed@airspeedskateparks.com
airspeedskateparks.com

CA Skateparks, Design / Build and
General Contracting
273 North Benson Avenue
Upland, California 91786
562-208-4646
skatedesign.com

Dreamland Skateparks, Gridline Inc.
4056 23rd Avenue SW
Seattle, Washington 98106
206-933-7915
gridline.com

Freshpark / Radius 8, Inc.
5900 Hollis Street, Suite S
Emeryville, California 94608-2008
800-490-2709
info@freshpark.com
freshpark.com

Ramptech
ramptech.com

RCMC Custom Cement Skateparks
rcmcsk8parks.com

Spectrum Skatepark Creations, Ltd.
M/A 2856 Clifftop Lane
Whistler, B.C.
V0N 1B2 Canada
250-238-0140
design@spectrum-sk8.com
spectrum-sk8.com

Team Pain
864 Gazelle Trail
Winter Springs, Florida 32708
407-695-8215
tim@teampain.com
teampain.com

John Woodstock Designs
561-743-5963
johnwoodstock@msn.com
woodstockskateparks.com

Videos / instructional

411 Video Productions. The First Step.

411 Video Productions. The Next Step.

Hawk, Tony. Tony Hawk's Trick Tips
Volume I: Skateboarding Basics. 900
Films, 2001.

Hawk, Tony. Tony Hawk's Trick Tips
Volume II: Essentials of Street. 900
Films, 2001.

Thrasher Magazine. How to
Skateboard. San Francisco, California:
High Speed Productions, Inc., 1995.

Thrasher Magazine. How to
Skateboard Better. San Francisco,
California: High Speed Productions,
Inc., 1997.

Transworld Skateboarding. Starting
Point. Oceanside, California, 1997.

Transworld Skateboarding. Trick Tips
with Wily Santos. Oceanside,
California, 1998.

Transworld Skateboarding. Starting
Point Number Two. Oceanside,
California, 1999.

Web sites

exploratorium.edu/skateboarding
Glossary, scientific explanations and
equipment for skating.

interlog.com/~mbrooke/skategeezer.ht
ml
International Longboarder magazine.

ncdsa.com
Northern California Downhill
Skateboarding Association.

skateboard.com
Chat and messages.

skateboarding.com
Every skater's site by Transworld
Skateboarding magazine.

skateboards.org
Parks, shops and companies.

skatelab.com
One of Los Angeles area's largest indoor parks and world's largest skateboard museum.

smithgrind.com
Skate news wire.

stevebadillo.net
info@stevebadillo.net

switchmagazine.com
Switch Skateboarding Magazine.

tailtap.com
Your direct source for hard to find books and magazines.

thrashermagazine.com
A comprehensive site by Thrasher magazine.

More Web sites

360flip.com
alvaskates.com
answers.com
blackplaguewheels.com
blitzdistribution.com
board-crazy.co.uk
concretedisciple.com
crailtap.com
dvsskate.com
dwindle.com
ehow.com
everything2.com
experiencefestival.com
floridaskater.com
forheavenskate.com
furytruckcompany.com
glidemagazine.com
how2skate.com
imdb.com
juicemagazine.com
kellylynn.com
kidzworld.com
mayaskates.com
myspace.com
ollieair.com
podiumdist.com
premise.tv
rainbowskateparks.com
rodneymullen.net
ruggedelegantliving.com
scholastic.com
secretsofsuccess.com
sk8ips.com

sk8kings.com
skateamerica.com
skateboarddirectory.com
skateboarder2.com
skatelab.com
skatelegends.com
skatepunk.net
skateshooters.com
socalskateparks.com
stevesteadham.com
tailtap.com
thinkquest.org
tonyhawk.com
twsbiz.com
wikihow.com
wikipedia.org
youtube.com

Steve's sponsors

Black Plague Wheels
85 Mahogany Lane
Simi Valley, CA 93065
818-439-2683
blackplaguewheels.com

DVS Shoe Company
955 Francisco Street
Torrance, California 90502
dvsshoes.com
dvsskate.com

Santa Monica Airlines Skateboards
3435 Ocean Park Blvd. #107/151
Santa Monica, CA 90405
smaskateboards.com

SkateLab
4226 Valley Fair St.
Simi Valley, California 93063
805-578-0040
skatelab.com

Index

Skateboarding: New Levels
Tips and Tricks for Serious Riders
Pro advice about gear, safety, mental
preparation and 25 tricks to know.
208 pages / 300 photos
1-884654-16-9 / $12.95

Skateboarding: Book of Tricks
Old school, new school and 34 tricks.
176 pages / 375 photos
1-884654-19-3 / $12.95

Skateboarding: Legendary Tricks
The fourth skateboarding guide by
Steve Badillo covers famous tricks
and the legendary riders who created
them.
192 pages / 600 photos
1-884654-30-4 / $12.95

Books by Steve Badillo and Tracks Publishing are available through all major booksellers in stores and on the Internet.

Doug Werner is the author or co-author of all eleven books in the Start-Up Sports® series. His publishing company, Tracks, is the world's leading producer of skate instructional guides. He lives in San Diego, California.

TRACKS

Our sport instructional guides are best-sellers because each book contains hundreds of images, is packed with expert advice and retails at a great price. No one else comes close.

Start-Up Sports® tackles the hottest sports. Forthright. Simple.
— Library Journal

trackspublishing.com

Steve Badillo has authored or co-authored five best-selling skateboarding guides including *Skateboarder's Start-Up, Skateboarding: New Levels, Skateboarding: Book of Tricks, Skateboarding: Legendary Tricks* and *Skateboarding: Legendary Tricks 2.*

Steve is a sponsored pro skater, runs the renowned SkateLab Skate Camp near Los Angeles, and has worked as a stunt double and actor in numerous commercials and films featuring skateboarding including *Lords of Dogtown.*

He is the head judge for the National High School Skateboard Association, a nationwide skateboarding program for high schools.

stevebadillo.net